ONCE WAS A BOY

Theo Dorgan

DEDALUS PRESS

ONCE WAS A BOY

First published in 2023 by
The Dedalus Press
13 Moyclare Road
Baldoyle
Dublin D13 K1C2
Ireland

www.dedaluspress.com

ISBN 978-1-915629-13-5 (paperback)
ISBN 978-1-915629-12-8 (hardback)

Dedalus Press titles are available in Ireland
from Argosy Books (www.argosybooks.ie) and in the UK
from Inpress Books (www.inpressbooks.co.uk)

Cover image: Linocut by Gaetano Tranchino
www.gaetanotranchino.com

The Dedalus Press receives financial assistance from
The Arts Council / An Chomhairle Ealaíon.

Contents

～

IT STARTS FROM HOME

～

CONVENT DAYS

∾

CODA

for Mick Hannigan
unswerving friend

IT STARTS FROM HOME

Bells break on the morning air ...

Bells break on the morning air, boom of the North Cathedral,
the rippling tones from Shandon. The tolling is low. That means
a funeral. Nobody we know, I would have heard the talk. Rolling over
the wrong notes, I pick out *Danny Boy*, her favourite song.

Sometimes, if I'm close, she folds me to her shoulder when it comes
on the radio. Face powder, Pond's cold cream. I don't remark the tears
when they come. She misses her mother and father. Inside the radio
as the valves heat up, the very particular smell of electricity.

In some discarded comic or magazine, the New York skyline at night.
I think of this when I watch the valves heat up, prompting feelings
I can't understand. The smooth Bakelite case has rounded corners.
Once I tried counting the ribs on the tuning knob until my eyes
	blurred.

Circling the mixing bowl with a finger, mock-reprimanded, I close
	my eyes
and try to distinguish flour from egg in the mixture. I filch a slice
	of apple,
bite, the sourness puckering my cheeks. I dip the slice in sugar,
	bite again.
The others have gone up the garden, almost I taste the ticking
	of the clock.

Sun-bubbles in the back door paint, white dust in the deep reveals.
Fingertips trailing the pebble dash as I walk around to the front,
at the right speed I make each separate finger hop and skip.
Braille, I think. Morse code. Words without content from a book.

Creak of the gate hinge …

Creak of the gate hinge, sharp and clear through the bustle
of brothers and sisters chattering and calling. Snap of the lid
on the teapot, rush of water as someone refills the kettle.
Soft flap of envelopes on tile, the letterbox cracks shut.

Once, when something had to be signed for, silent beside her
as my mother reached for his pen, I caught the acrid whiff
of age and sweat from his heavy uniform, the rank
smell of clothes brought in damp from the line.

He hefts the heavy bag on its leather strap. Canvas
will snag a nail, warms when you brush your hand across it,
a wave of heat in the cup of your palm. If it's like the strap
on my sandals, it's furry on one side, soft to the gliding thumb.

For no particular reason, I lick the windowpane. Metallic,
I hadn't expected that. Back of the hand to clear my tongue.
Nothing. How strange that something should taste of nothing.
Right now I would like to bite deep into an orange, or an apple.

Outside Twomey's, someone has stopped the postman, is holding
his bike for him while, hat cocked, he fans through a fistful of letters.
He plucks an envelope from the bunch, squints, then hands it over.
Against the red of her coat, for just a moment, white shape of a
    letterbox.

A light wind comes up …

A light wind comes up, tang of roasting barley from Murphy's Brewery.
Cut in with this, on a bad day, the sour copper of blood from
    Denny's Cellar.
I prefer slaughterhouse, relishing the word, its weight. Cellar's for wine,
for mustiness, mildew and damp. Room under a tavern in
    Treasure Island.

Clip-clip of a shears, one of the Twomeys trimming the privet hedge.
Vincey, probably, nearest in age to me, and bored by the sound of it.
Steady and regular, my father says, keeping the rhythm helps you
    cut clean.
He stops and starts, clack and a silence then an irritated blurring rush.

The farther you look, the deeper the haze. Sergeant Moroney
    across the road
painted his house last week, it's crisp and clean. Down by the
    brewery the roof
ridges are blurring, and farther down into the heart of the city
    spires and domes
are shimmering through a rolling, shifting fog, lit from the inside
    with river light.

I pluck a grass blade and rip it through my teeth, the bitter milky sap.
Ellen comes from the shop, bread in the bag so fresh I can taste it.
Madge Harrington's penny ice-pops for all — she makes them by
    freezing
cordial in egg cups. Suck the raspberry out, the null taste of the ice.

I tip the lawnmower on its side, knurled wheel spins freely but the
    blades
are stiff. Crusted grass dried on the axles, my finger will turn a
    faded green.

The can is white and black and red; I carefully squeeze out lucent oil, slow, steady.

The blades whir as they spin; oil drips on the concrete path, soaks in black.

From the soft fog of the morning …

From the soft fog of the morning
rolling past and over me
I pluck your flat cap
and bring it to my face.
Brylcreem and pipe smoke,
the wool weave still holding
its original smell, faint as
the smell of your sweat.

You take the rolled cap
from your jacket pocket, settle
it firmly on your head. Left foot
on the pedal, you hop once,
twice, then swing the other leg
smoothly over and push down.
A glance over your shoulder
and then you're off.

I open the window and listen —
that faint squeak as you gather speed,
tick and hum of the chain.
So quiet the morning, each sound
distinct in its own bubble of air:
sparrows chittering in the hedge,
a van down in the valley accelerates,
a motorbike growling soft and low.

I dress by touch, yesterday's clothes,
cotton of T-shirt, bobbled wool
of jumper, obdurate knotted laces
to be teased open, re-tied in a bow.

Door handle warmer than toilet flush,
colder than tap. He'd have run
hot water for shaving.
The ribbed handle of his safety razor.

Slightly burned toast, taste catches
in my throat. The spoonful of milk left
in the bowl when the cornflakes are gone.
Tea with milk and sugar,
tannic aftertaste on the teeth.
From the soft fog of the sea, a swell
bears up into the light of morning,
for just a moment, your flat cap.

From the soft fog of this afternoon ...

From the soft fog of this afternoon
rolling over me, Olympian, reflective,
I sift the images with a trailing hand,
feeling for sparks of energy and light.
I breathe air and ozone when I surface,
consider a moment what I've found
then sink again, unhurried and calm,
into the blue-grey of what passes.

What was immediate then, immediate now.
What was far under and lost,
or so I thought, still pulses rich with life.
That boy so vivid in his living moment.
The bells break through, silver and bronze,
sending waves of light up to the hills,
down in a spreading flood through the city valley.

He dismounts, unzips his coat, takes off
his cap and rolls it carefully, stows it
in the right hand jacket pocket.
Pipe and tobacco, matches, in the left.
At the back door, wiping her hands in her apron,
she greets him with a soft kiss.
Clatter of dishes from the kitchen,
an excitement of brothers and sisters.

I am all attention when they turn to look at me,
their blue eyes rich with acceptance.
She makes a small gesture with her hand,
I run to their awkward embrace but there's
that hesitation, the wrench when I break
from my own bubble into theirs. And they see it.

She kisses the top of my sun-warm head,
he ruffles my hair. Close as we ever will be.

The sea closes over us, warm and cottony
as light fog. It bears us on, and up, and out.
Heat in her cupped palm, closing on mine.
She spins away into the flow, letting me go.
I strike a match, shielding it from the breeze;
he inhales, the sweet tobacco smoulders,
he fades in the weave of smoke. Her hand,
his flat cap, plucked for a moment from the swell.

I had the thought before I knew the words ...

I had the thought before I knew the words. Alien. Other.
New clothes, new coat, a leather bag, pencils. New shoes.
I'd seen them go by the gate, some stumbling out, some clutching
a mother's hand (*mother*, I noted) and I saw doubt, distress,
and something more — I saw that after a while they marched
by themselves, (*beside* not *with* their mothers), I had the thought
but not the words, that clear distinction. I knew it would come to this
for me, too, in time. And then the time came.

September air, crisp, not cold yet, curious at how I felt — new clothes,
new shoes, that particular pleasure — wary but interested.
A hug as he left for work (*that's new;*) her sad excitement,
her new hat. A look up from the bottom step at the silent house
and I knew. I was outside home now, nothing would ever be the same.

CONVENT DAYS

First Day

The gate set deep, the steps go left and up.
My mother is wearing a hat, I have new shoes.
Boys with their mothers behind and before us.

This woman is to be called Mrs. Ryan,
She smells of flowers, her eyes are kind.
I follow her into a room filling up with boys.

Some are crying, I consider this carefully.
Some try to run after their mothers, some
mothers are crying, too. Interesting.

There are drawings on the wall, chickens and houses.
Rows of seats, these are called desks where we
sit and stare around us, scuffing our feet.

It's all very dusty and noisy, then the door closes.
This Mrs. Ryan, we are to give her our attention.
She says we will learn letters and numbers but

first we will draw. Crayons and large sheets of paper,
big girls in dark dresses move through the room, red
ties around their waists. Men wear them around their necks.

I will be here tomorrow, and the next day, and the next
for, my father said last night, years.
This is school, she says, you come here to learn things.

Nuns

We are chanting our numbers when the door opens,
one of the women all dressed in black comes in,
her dress trails whispers on the bare floor boards.

Her smile is kind, she looks around at us while
she speaks to Mrs. Ryan. I like that she looks at me
looking up at her and crinkles her eyes.

Mrs. Ryan calls her Sister Angela.
The bell at twelve o'clock is called the Angelus.
We have to stand up when we pray.

A big man with a round face and white hair comes,
he helps us with our painting. We paint with our fingers —
chickens, houses. We can take the paintings home.

In the yard, Jimmy Daly says the man is his uncle.
I have an uncle, Uncle John, but I don't know
if he could come in here. The women in black are

called nuns, they walk up and down the yard,
staring at us. Some of them scare me,
they have hard eyes and their hands are hidden.

One wall of the yard is high and red, but
not as high as the big school. Girls' voices
come falling down loud from the open windows.

We run up and down between wall and school,
shouting and pushing, running, running.
Up and back. Over and across. The gate is closed.

When it's time to go back, somebody rings a bell.
One-two, one-two. The bell is heavy, the girl ringing it
has her face all squeezed up, that's how I know.

Closed In

I know the gate is closed because I tried it.
We have to stay inside all day. Inside the yard.
Inside the room. After a while the room smells

and we can have the window open. I drag my nails
across the ribbed desk, making them skip as I press.
I lean back and stare at the ceiling. Two bare bulbs.

Can I bring my ball to school? No. My hurley? No.
Can I bring my Dinky cars? You're not supposed to.
Hand in my pocket, I spin and spin the wheels.

The worst is when we have to pretend to sleep.
Palms of our hands flat on the warm wood.
Arms folded, heads down. Mrs. Ryan reads,

I know this because if you very slowly slide your head
on the backs of your hands, a small bit, another bit,
you can see her desk. This is called squinting.

After the sleep we have letters or numbers.
I already know the names of days. On Fridays
we have a story, then we go home for two days.

Back Again

Then we have to go back again. Monday.
My Dad is putting his bike into the shed.
I don't think I'll bother going back, I say.

He sits on his heels and looks at me. Back where,
he says. School. Oh and why's that, he asks.
Well, to be honest, it isn't very interesting.

He starts roaring laughing and so do my Mam,
Aunt Angela, Uncle John. I don't understand
but it makes me angry and confused.

You just have to knuckle down, he says, ruffles
my hair and takes a wrapped sweet from his pocket.
When they've gone inside, I squat on the hot concrete

and grind my knuckles into the ground.
I learn nothing from this except that it hurts.
Why tell me something that makes no sense?

Chalk

Chalk is confusing, greasy and dusty all at once.
It comes in sticks, packed into cardboard boxes
like soldiers. Mostly it's white, sometimes it's coloured.

With chalk you can write on the stones they call slates.
We are writing out numbers and letters with little pieces,
Mrs. Ryan breaks up the big sticks and hands out the bits.

You rub out what you've written, dust on your sleeve,
the dust makes you sneeze, then you write on the slate again.
We do this over and over. For a while.

We liven up when she hands out the coloured bits
and lets us draw. You can smudge the colours together.
She makes us rub everything out when we've finished.

Only some boys are sent to the cupboard for the chalk.
Only some boys are told to open the window or close it.
I like feeling important. Me, Daly, Evans, Mullane.

One of the boys who's always crying hits me.
This is in the yard when the nun has her back turned.
Mullane hits the boy, then we're all hitting each other.

Well, I think afterwards, after they've separated us,
at least that was interesting. But also, and this is a new thing,
I'm afraid of that boy now. He wants to hurt me.

Rocking Horse

Taller than any of us, the rocking horse in the corner.
Black and shiny, grey patches all over, a hairy tail,
and hair on its neck, too. It rocks backward and forward,

it makes a creaky sound when it's pushed. The eyes are red
and yellow; they look angry, they look far away
at something way out beyond the blackboard.

What I don't understand is this: Mrs Ryan will pick you up
and give you a go on the rocking horse if you've been good.
But, she'll do the same for one of the cry-babies — what's that

about? At home, when I'm good I am petted and praised.
When I break something, when I won't do what I'm told,
they scold me. What my Aunt calls *giving out.*

This though, with the rocking horse, I can't make sense of it.
What is it, Jimmy Daly asks me. Are you all right?
I shake my head, I'm grand. Shove doubt back down.

Home, bouncing a ball in the yard, I think about this.
Why did he ask me that? Ah.
Must have been something in my face.

So what's talking inside shows on the outside.
I'm staring into space when Mam,
coming out to hang up the washing, says penny for them.

For what? For your thoughts, she says, what you're thinking.
Thoughts. What you're saying to yourself that nobody hears
except you. All that is called thinking. Can you buy them?

I'd like a penny. Pineapple bars are my favourite, they're a penny. Don't know what else for a penny. But she's laughing, that means it's a joke. Anyway, she's gone on up the steps with the wet clothes.

We Move Up a Class

We move up a class, one more to go.
We accept everything we are told. There is God,
who looks after everything and knows when we're bold.

There is his mother, and her son who is Jesus.
We have bits of this from home. The picture
of the man with his heart on the outside is Jesus.

Jesus died for our sins. We make it up to him
when we say prayers and by being good.
The mother of Jesus is Mary, we sing to her

and these songs are called hymns. She has an altar
in every classroom, we sneak looks when a door is open
and we think ours has much nicer flowers.

The black nuns are holy, this means special to God.
When you kneel down bits of dirt on the floor hurt your knees.
You join your hands, lift up your face, eyes closed.

The black nuns have their arms folded always,
their hands hidden away. Not like the mother of Jesus,
they have faces that don't smile. Except for Sister Angela.

Next year we have Sister Angela, this year we have Miss Coffey.
She bosses us around. She has a loud hard voice.
She slaps people for being wrong, or bold.

She picks on people. One boy has German Measles.
When he comes back she makes him stand on his desk.
She pinched him behind the knees. Now, she said,

how do you like Irish Measles. He starts crying
and she slaps him for crying. We know this is wrong.
We look around at each other, no need to say. We know.

Learning to Read

We are learning to read. Black signs on a white page.
Now I am not in the room if I don't want to be.
Now I can have a dog, a rich father and mother,

we can have a car, an apple tree, a stream in the garden.
Now I can be in places where everything comes out right.
Where men have horses and guns and swords

and the boys are always winning their fights. The sun shines
and when it rains there are big log fires and mugs of cocoa.
There are rivers for catching fish and high mountains to climb,

long trips by train through fields of corn, or journeys
by sea, these I like best of all, with the wind howling
and all the sails big and white and full of the wind

and the boy is brave, he steers the ship by the big wheel
all through the storm with the Captain by his side
and never once, not even once, is he afraid.

And it isn't all made up, like the stories my Dad reads out to me.
I can read about stars, jungles, dinosaurs, other countries
and what grows there, what people do, what an orchestra is

and what makes an engine work, the names of places —
India, Russia, China, Japan — where people wear clothes
that are different from ours and where they eat strange food.

Maybe best of all is that I remember what I read. It all goes on.
When the clock is moving so slowly, when I've done my sums
and I'm staring out the window, fidgeting and trapped,

I can be back in yesterday's book, riding my pony with cowboys
or driving a race car or hiding from pirates in a cave and,
if Miss Coffey doesn't catch me, flying, free as a seagull.

Quarant'ore

We wind up through the grounds in a long procession,
we are going to the chapel in the middle of the day.
We walk in twos, no talking, anyone talking gets a slap

when we are back in class. We talk without moving our lips,
we wonder what's going on. The chapel is red brick,
white stone around pointy windows, around the polished door.

Inside it isn't a bit like Blackpool Church. All polished wood,
it smells like flowers, and there are low walls between the three parts.
We are on the left. In the middle, we see their heads, all nuns

praying out loud together. Beyond the nuns, where we can't see,
other voices rising and falling, women's voices.
The tabernacle is white and shining and complicated

with small gold doors in the middle and big candles lighting.
The altar boy's cassock is black, his surplice is white —
Aunt Angela always teasing, what's the word for this, for that?

The priest wears a long cape, gold and shining.
They walk to the altar steps, they bow, the priest says Latin words
and the nuns answer. We don't know Latin. Latin is a dead language.

Sister Magdalene has been teaching us a hymn. Now she signals
and we stand up, she counts to four by chopping her hand
and we all begin to sing. The nuns join in, the women too.

It makes the hair stand up on your neck when everybody sings.
I think these must be the women who work in the laundry.
The nuns have high voices, even the old ones sound young.

At the end of it all the priest turns with what is called the monstrance
and holds it up high, it looks like the sun with a small window in
the middle.
Inside is 'the sacred host, children, the body and blood of Our Lord.'

Kneeling, we bless ourselves and somebody whispers 'monsterance'.
Even though this is a bit like mass and serious, everyone sniggers.
Sister Magdalene says 'ciúnas'. This is an Irish word and it means
'quiet'.

It also means we are all going to get slapped when we get back.
There's another thing about reading,
you learn that words can mean more than what they mean.

Hell

Nothing funny, our last year, preparing for first communion
when all the talk is of our black souls, the fires of hell,
the rebel angels, the sin of disobedience. Sister Benedicta

is plump and jolly but her smiles die at her eyes. Imagine,
she says, holding your palm over a candle flame for just a second,
and now imagine that burning pain for all eternity. For ever and ever.

Nightmares for weeks, unable to sleep for terror. Don't think
about it, my mother says. Easy to say, but how do you do that?
It isn't the burning, it's my mind struggling with for ever and ever.

Grey blue void of terror, columns of ghostly numbers marching
towards and over and past me and I have nowhere to go,
there is nothing to see and nobody else at all to hear me plead.

Neither awake nor asleep, no way to tell, but now I wake to the gate
below creaking, my father leaving for work, the rattle of water
filling the kettle, and I have to wash, dress and somehow go on

as if this is all right, as if tonight again it won't all start over.
How do you tell the smell, the taste, the touch of such things?
What's wrong with you these days? Nothing, I have to go.

When you die, when you're good you go to heaven, she says,
Sister Benedicta who has three hairs on her chin. Heaven,
it seems, has angels, and clouds of light, and harp music.

For ever and ever. Hell, she says, her eyes are bright, her pink tongue
sticking out now, hell is devils with pitchforks and horrible smells and
flames burning you on and on and on forever. She closes her eyes.

In the yard at break, grabbing small bottles of milk from the iron crate, Mick Evans leans over and asks me, what's a pitchfork? Don't know. Heaven doesn't sound all that great, he says. I was just thinking the same.

Did you see the three hairs on her chin? I did. Then someone drops a Dinky on the ground and we're all scuffling and pushing to get a hold of it. The girl with the bell appears, we line up to go back in.

Confession

Before Communion there is First Confession. For weeks we rehearse —
how to examine your conscience, which means remember the bad things
you did, then the first words: bless me Father for I have sinned.

They march us to the Cathedral for this. Everyone calls it the
      North Chapel
but Sister Benedicta insists on Cathedral. We line up on the long seats
then one by one we open the door, step into the dark, kneel.

All in one long rushed sentence: I was disobedient to my parents,
I used bad language, twice father, I wasn't paying attention in school.
The word has been passed around, always you start with disobedient.

What did you get, Jimmy Daly whispers from behind joined hands.
Three Hail Mary's and an Our Father, you? The same he says.
Seems fair to me, we all have the same penance for the same sins.

My mother's eyes on me are amused as she walks me home.
Well, do you feel all holy now, after confessing your sins?
I can't see me going to Hell, I say, and the laughter comes gushing out.

Wait'll I tell you what this fella just said, she tells Mrs. Driscoll,
sweeping the path outside her gate. Now they are both laughing
and I am annoyed, I don't see what's funny. Which makes them
      laugh more.

I wish I could laugh at what's waiting in the dark, burrowing down
into the woolly blankets, watching the streetlight sway and dance
across the ceiling. The marching numbers, the cold blue-grey cloud.

Communion Day

White socks and sandals, white shorts,
a white V-neck over a stiff white shirt.
A red tie, white jacket that's called a blazer.
My neck still sore from yesterday's razored haircut.

We march to the North Chapel from the school,
all of us with a rosette pinned to our blazers,
a holy medal in the middle jumps a bit as you walk.
The North Chapel is full, our parents of course,
and a great crowd of old women

gawking at us. The lore has us busy
figuring the money we hope to make
from visits to aunts, neighbours,
grandmothers, but Benedicta is hissing
as we file into our seats: remember now,
don't chew Holy God.

The priest puts the white wafer on my tongue,
I wonder does he ever get spit on his fingers,
and I go back to my seat, the host curved
to the roof of my mouth. I spend the mass
trying to ease it down, swallow.

Now I have God inside me, I tell myself,
testing the thought. I don't feel
any different though. All right then.
I suppose that's that.
Mam has a new hat, a new handbag.
She's pink and happy and excited.

It's all go in the big yard outside,
the sun is shining, people I don't know
are pressing coins into my hand
and we haven't even started our visiting.
Cake, lemonade, talk, a shilling or a half-crown,
we move on to the next.

My Grandfather's is best.
He owns a small sweetshop and takes
a Patsi Pop, dunks it in fizzy orange
until the ice and the ice-cream foam,
then subside in the glass. A ten-shilling note
folded with mock discretion

into my hand, a wink and a gruff laugh
when I try to hug him.
Go on with you now, he says,
don't spend it all in the one shop.
Say a prayer for us now, he says
when we're leaving. As if I have power.

I hand over the money to Mam
as we leave each house.
Not to mind, to keep.

Rebel Angel

Bomber Murphy is good at fighting and running around,
is always getting slapped for something. His shirt buttons
often gapped & wrong. He doesn't always comb his hair.

I'd be afraid of him except that for some reason he likes me,
is always telling me things. He brings in birds' eggs to show us,
conkers, curious things he finds on the street, bits of machines.

Bomber knows things none of us know. You see them women,
he says, that you see Sundays out walking with them blue berets on?
Them are called penitents, all bad girls only the nuns took them in,

they work in the laundry to say they're sorry. For how long, I ask,
tracing the rough red stone of the wall. For how long what?
For how long do they have to stay? I dunno. Forever?

Up Peacock Lane there's a wooden door in the long convent wall.
People are always coming and going, carrying bags up to the door,
collecting brown paper parcels. Getting the sheets washed, says
    Bomber.

We wash our own, I tell him, you should see the line when my Mam
hangs out the sheets. Like the sails on a sailing ship, I tell him.
We've only a yard, he says. There wouldn't be room.

There's an afternoon with the sun high and it's October cold
when Sister Angela, we're in her class now, sends Mullane and myself
out to bring Bomber back to school. He's on the hop.

I'm impressed with Sister Angela's thinking. Mullane is big and strong,
stronger than Bomber, I'm the one is supposed to talk him into it.
Faced with the two of us he comes cheerfully enough, considering.

Miss Coffey would have slapped him, but Sister Angela just ruffles
   his hair.

Ah, she says, *my rebel angel.* Any more than Mullane, I can't figure
   this out.

No more than I understand why the whole business makes me uneasy.

Prize

Last class before we pile out into the summer.
The room is giddy and spinning, light flashing in the high windows.
The prizes are laid out solemnly on the teacher's desk.

I covet the football, heavy rubber, not like those flyway plastic ones
that the wind takes and you can't predict where it will fall.
First prize is me. I hesitate, then go for the holy picture.

The nun is surprised, my pals whispering urgently the football,
    the football,
but I was in trouble leaving the house, the picture will soften the air.
You're mad, what did you do that for? I won't answer them, stubborn.

This is for you, I say. Flour on her hands, she's smudging the glass
but I bite my tongue. Did you pick this out? Eyes to the ground,
I nod yes. What else could you have picked? A football.

I can hear a bee buzzing in the cool kitchen. Maybe it's a bluebottle.
She cuffs me softly on the back of the head, you're a right rogue, what
am I rearing at all? I finger-brush my hair, the dust dancing in the
    sunlight.

I climb through the barbed wire and head up the Bishop's Field,
beating at thistles and nettles with my hurley. I stop and stare up
    at the sky,
seeing, back there in the classroom, me making that cold
    calculation.

Coming Events

The steps up to the cross are steep and warm to the palm.
I climb on to the broad platform, lean my back on the upright,
its life-size Jesus of polished stone, his head heavy and hanging down.

If he lifted his head he'd see the great chimney of Murphy's Brewery
rising up out of the valley — how I imagine a lighthouse.
The haze all down into the city could be the sea, and the city

could have sunk under the waves years ago and we sailed into it
from America, me on the wheel, with a great crowd of pirates
and desperate characters all hungry for gold and treasure.

Away over the hedge at the end of the playing field behind me,
the grey roof, the big ugly chimneys of the Brothers' house.
The North Monastery, next step in the life sentence of school.

According to someone's big brother, they beat you all the time there,
No nuns, no women teachers, only big cranky men from the country
in long black robes. Beat you for anything at all, them and their leathers.

Cassocks, I said, those are probably cassocks, sure aren't the Brothers
next best to priests. Stands to reason they'd be wearing priest clothes.
Are you listening to me at all, what're you on about, cassocks?

Spit in the corners of his mouth. You'd want to be thinking about
    the leather,
don't go getting smart with them boyos. Mrs. Ryan comes to my mind.
The good boys and the bold boys, all taking turns on the rocking horse.

BOYS' PRIMARY SCHOOL

Storm Warning

It's like being at a match when some team is surging for goal,
the rising wave of noise as I step through the gates into the tunnel,
then up the ramp. The roar of boys, summer put down,

all over the wide-open yard, opening their lungs to autumn,
the closing in of the walls. I am intimidated, and why wouldn't
you be, I ask myself, smallest boy here. Everything new.

Maybe I read too much during the holidays. The words are
awkward, shaping themselves in my head, testing the distance
between what I feel now and what I'm supposed to be.

I know to be careful here, to mask what's inside from punches
and pushing, rough tackling, grunts and intimidation, chaos
everyone else seems to understand. Rules I can't seem to grasp.

Out of the storm, a handful of known faces. I hitch the new schoolbag
tight to my shoulders, smelling new leather, push through the crowd.
I'm not the only one fearful, we talk in low voices, scanning it all.

A bell sounds out, vigorous, clattery, and the boys rush to form ranks,
arranging themselves, shouldering and shoving. We huddle together
until a tall Brother come striding towards us in the deepening silence.

We understand that when the bell goes we, too, are to gather into a
   square.
We watch them march off, each class led by a teacher. No women
   to be seen.
The Brother surveys us, hands on his hips, eyes sharp, black-framed
   glasses.

A man in a grey suit comes towards us, a list in his hand. He calls
    out names,
we shuffle to join one group or another. This is to be my class, I see,
relieved that they are mostly boys I know. Although one or two of them

have it in for me. Never mind that, I don't like the cut of him, this
    teacher.
We haven't even started and already he looks cross. Carey, someone
    whispers,
my brother says cranky in the mornings, you have to watch out
    for him.

The Lore

Some unfamiliar faces here. I take a seat halfway back,
the row by the window. Avoid the front row, the lore says.
Also the back row, they're wise to lads who hide at the back.

Anseo, we answer when Carey calls our names from the roll.
He calls out the names in Irish, and some boys struggle to recognise
the unfamiliar form. The irritated look on his face when he's forced

to repeat himself. I see him note those boys, am uneasy for them.
Don't draw attention unless it's to give the right answer to a question.
We absorb the word instantly, passed down through mystery channels,

never questioned. We have more faith in the lore than in the Catechism.
How to be safe, how to avoid being beaten, how to disappear.
Bright hard sun through the high windows, quick energies of
    the boys

all around me; there's fizz of expectation, backwash of summer spent
running free and wild. Carey surveys us grimly, and then he smiles.
The shock steadies the room. I sit up straight, what's this now?

Ah lads, he says, settle down, settle down. A grand day like this,
ye'd prefer to be running wild after a football, or climbing trees,
or maybe a day on the beach, hah? Am I right? But winter's coming,

lads, aren't ye better off here in the warm, out of the rain,
    learning things
that will stand to ye when ye're grown up? Isn't it for your own good?
Now, out with the copybooks and we'll see what ye're like at the writing.

I'm at the dining room table, copying out sentences, when Dad comes home.

What's the new teacher like, he asks. I put my pen down, think about it.

He seems all right, I say. But I wouldn't trust him an inch.

Asking for It

I hold my hand out flat, palm turned up,
thumb well out of the way.
The trouble with you, mister —*slap* —
is that you're too smart — *slap* —
for your own good — *slap*. Now back
to your seat and mind that tongue of yours.

Sweeney beside me can't figure out
long division, asked for the answer.
Carey caught me whispering.
You, boy, what are you whispering about?
Nothing, Sir. Nothing, nothing?
D'you think I'm a fool, boy? I don't know, Sir.

You were asking for it, the consensus at break,
what did you go and say that for?
I don't know, I just said the words that
came into my head. Bomber shakes his head,
sorrowful. Never provoke 'em, he says, never.
We know his father beats him.

Carey is talking to the tall red-headed Brother,
their eyes tracking the yard.
I note their cold amusement and look away.
Shaken, feeling my back go stiff:
my hand still hurts, a dull pain like you feel
after you've banged your elbow.

If the edge of the leather strikes on the base
of the thumb, that's what you feel —
the lingering throb after the shock wears off.

The wisdom says, always offer your left,
it's hard to write for a while after
if you give them your right. Somebody asked,

but what if you're left-handed? I join in
the jeering, happy to sink into gang mind,
but partly I'm dislocated, remembering
the afternoon we brought Bomber in.
Bright and clear. Sister Angela ruffling his hair.
My rebel angel she called him, and I half-understood.

Duress

The plucky British officer is confronting
his Japanese captors. Prisoner of war,
erect, surrounded by bayonets: I will not
answer your questions under duress,
he says. I put *The Victor* down, reach
for the dictionary, look it up. Duress.

I know 'plucky' already, from Treasure Island,
I know it's the right word for him.
Adjective, a word that colours a noun.
What would be a good adjective for
that red-headed Brother? And why
am I thinking of him, here by the fire,

homework done, the radio on low,
Dad with *The Echo*, Mam upstairs
putting the youngest to bed? Sometimes,
what you're thinking about is more real
than what's right in front of you,
more real than hungry, or warm, or cold.

They call it daydreaming in school, they beat you
for it if you get caught. But, what do they expect,
when you know the spellings, you've done the sums,
you're waiting for the others to finish?
What is it that bothers them?
I look at the word again. Duress.

They look at me as if I've grown an extra head,
my pals at the gate, impatient to get home.
But sure you have to go to school, one says,

you just have to. How would we learn anything?
Yeah, but why do they have to beat us all the time?
What good does that do?

Dunno, someone says, that's just the way it is
I suppose. Anyway, sure what can you do?
Then it's all forgotten as we're shoved aside
by some bigger lads coming out the gate
and we're off down the hill at full gallop,
all heading for home in God's fresh air.

Class Collection

We collect for the Black Babies,
something to do with missions in Africa.
He tallies the count by rows, whichever row
gives the most gets homework off
for the weekend. A new boy joins us,
a couple of weeks in. We see his father

drop him off at the gate. We note the big car.
We note that he's a bit nervous.
I don't know that anything was exactly said,
but we quickly grow fond of Martin,
his large contributions to the collection
easing his path to acceptance.

The word says that Carey pockets the money;
we're not sure if we believe this
but we spread the word anyway.
A certain grim satisfaction in this quiet revenge.
Truth be told, I don't mind the homework,
but it's a given among us to hate it

and I'm happy to go with the gang.
A balance against the grey fog in my head,
of something inside me that holds back
from the whirl of cliques. Seriously,
someone asked, you read stuff you don't have
to read? The gap is already there,

and I have a new skill to learn, masking
my sense of distance from what's taken
as given by most. Take Martin for instance —

I am gleeful as anyone in the rough
crowding that has him give, and give,
but I feel his unease, I see the knot in his tie

that he's always adjusting. Our pennies,
we're told, go to help the priests in Africa
set up schools for poor children. I wonder
if they're like us, with our patched jumpers,
our scuffed shoes, except that of course
they probably don't have to wear as much

because, it's a given, we are poor,
and some of us are poorer than others.
Except for Martin, and there's the thing,
the reason some bully him, some ignore him
and others are fascinated: imagine, they have a car!
I squint up at Carey, counting coins. He has a car.

Terrazzo

The corridors are long, the floors of coloured
and polished stone, curved up
to meet the walls, edged with a line of gold.
I'm outside the cloakroom, sent
on some errand, staring down the long
perspective when the tall Brother appears.

He knows my name. What are you looking at?
The floor, Brother, the floor, is that marble?
Marble, he says, and he waits until I glance up.
Not marble, no, that is called terrazzo.
I repeat the word under my breath.
It's an Italian word, do you know where Italy is?

I stand straight: the capital of Italy is called Rome.
Italy is a Mediterranean country.
The Pope lives in Rome, and before him
Julius Caesar. The language is called Italian.
He keeps a straight face, what people say
when they mean trying not to laugh.

Where did he come from? I never saw him,
or heard him. Now he is actually smiling.
Well now, answer me this: why do you think
the walls along there are curved?
I don't think they are, Brother, I think
the floor curves up to the walls, d'ye see?

Fair point, he says, fair point — but why,
do you think? I suppose it's for mopping,
Brother, 'twould be much faster for mopping

if you didn't have to watch out for the walls.
Right enough, he says, now off with you,
Mr. Carey will be wondering where you are.

Hand on the classroom door I look down:
if you threw a bucket of water along the floor,
some of it would wash into the classroom.
Problem. I stare back down the corridor
and he holds my look, grins, turns away.
Well now, that fella doesn't miss much. *Terrazzo*.

Gymnastics

In the comics they are called plimsolls.
We call them rubber dollies. Why?
Nobody knows. Dad says it's a Cork name,
I didn't know we can do that,
change the name of a thing.
Gym shoes, the teacher says. White canvas,

we wear them for what is called gymnastics.
Vests, football shorts, we change
on the long benches around the wall.
I enjoy this, the stretches, jumping and running,
I enjoy it more than the football games
in the yard or on the street, especially sprints.

We buy them in Drummy's on Merchants Quay.
I expected ships, somehow, warehouses,
giant barrels of wine, horses and cranes
and great masts sparred and canvassed.
The name is the name of what used to be,
a disappointment in fact but later,

snug to the fire, I paint ships
and colours and exotic sailors into the name,
making the picture come alive.
Merchants, I think, must have looked like
Mr. Clifford who has a grocery shop
on Shandon Street, full of rich things.

The gym teacher used to be in the army.
He's keen on what he calls drill.
We have small coloured flags,

we make lines and we copy his movements.
He gets ratty when we don't all make
the same move at the same time,

he shouts and roars at us, but he doesn't
beat us. In our eyes, he's all right.
On Wednesday mornings there's a feeling
of lightness, packing the rubber dollies.
Today we have gymnastics, a small taste
of freedom inside the walls.

Exposure

I'm good at sums, I remember the Catechism
answers, I'm nearly always the best
at Irish and English compositions.
At Christmas I'm top of the class. I guessed
it was coming; the lore says
you should act surprised, make little of it,

don't be acting the big man, but I'm confused.
When some fella scores a goal
he's all over the place, roaring and boasting,
jumping in the air — so why walk
to the top of the class like I imagine
a condemned man walking to the gallows?

Because later, out in the yard or outside
the gate, someone is going to bump you,
maybe give you a dig, someone with his face
all twisted up will go: look at you,
you think you're a great fella, don't ya,
full of yourself? Maybe a kick in the shin,

your bag grabbed and thrown to the side
of the road. The night before they give out
the prizes, I lie in a half-dream puzzling
this out. It's like I'm floating under the classroom
ceiling, looking down. Carey has some boy by the ear,
shaking a copybook in his other hand.

You're a fool, boy, a fool, and that's all
you'll ever be all your life. If you're lucky
you'll end up down the docks, or driving a lorry,

if you're really lucky maybe they'll let you
sweep the floors down in Fords or Dunlops.
The boy is shrivelling up inside —

Shannon from Churchfield, quiet and slow-moving.
I see how this can build up inside,
the idea that you're good for nothing,
I want him to stand up straight, turn and give Carey
a dig in the gut. My brother wakes, asks
what's up, what did that pillow do to you?

No holy picture this time, I'm taking the football.
I avoid all eyes, walking up and back
but when they let us out early, pushing and jostling,
I turn from the gate and run back into the yard,
kicking the ball high in the air before me.
All of us swarming after, cheering.

Attitude

The long days, rain beating against
the high windows. I trace the patterns
where baked-on dust shapes river deltas,
vertical pools, lets rivulets run, and mostly
I don't get caught, having learned
to look sideways at the world outside.

In the cloakroom, our duffle coats hang
sodden and cold; if we're lucky
they will be half-dry when it's time
to go home. Passing the open door
I catch the smell from the butcher's
that time the fridge opened

and Mr. Buckley walked out, shouldering
a side of beef — behind him,
half-cloaked in the cloudy frost, a row
of carcases hung from brutal hooks.
Now, the smell of wet wool and body odours,
wet feet in the hot classroom.

You're hard on shoes, my mother says,
and I know it means she is worried
about the cost of repairs, or even replacement.
 You'll have to make do until
the next First Tuesday. I know this means
Children's Allowance Payment,

the money that keeps our heads above water.
Dear God, says Carey, you smell like
wild animals, do you never wash at home?

You, boy, open a window before
we suffocate. Cold heads, warm bodies
and wet feet — the man is a genius.

I know this is called sarcasm — I didn't know
it was called that until, I forget what prompted it,
Dad told me sharply not to be so sarcastic.
It's a bit odd, to have your mind forming words
and thoughts all by itself. If that's how it works.
Whatever, I'm getting used to it.

Attitude, there's another thing now.
I don't think I like your attitude, boy —
Carey to Billy Murray when Murray
 just shrugged and strolled back to his desk
after six with the leather. Got another two
for that, and shrugged again.

I'm thinking I might get an attitude myself,
seeing the way it provokes them.
All the long winter into spring we struggle
with boredom, repetition inside the walls
dulling our thoughts, the cold and the rain outside
making play all but impossible.

Dark when you wake, and near-dark
when you're going home. A fog in my mind
that only lifts when, brothers and sisters asleep,
the radio on low downstairs,
I tent the bedspread over my head
and lose myself, torch-lit, in a book.

Hymns

They have us singing hymns that make me
feel dreamy and slow. Hymns to Mary,
and the classroom feels different,
especially when we sing all standing together.

See us hurrying to school with armfuls of
lilac for the May altar, it makes me laugh —
all these hard chaws, the playground tough guys,
piling their offerings, grabbed out of gardens,
on the master's desk; all tongue-sticking-out
concentration as they push and shove

to settle the blue and white crepe paper,
to fill vases, arrange the flowers, so that our statue,
glowing up there in the top corner
away from the window, will be the best,
the one teachers and Brothers and other classes
will stop at the open door to admire.

May is the Month of Mary, we sing, our voices soft;
Hail, Queen of Heaven, we sing,
and I have a funny feeling in my chest, like
something's loosening, breaking open:
We sing only the first verse, but we sing it twice,
always louder the second time:

Hail Queen of Heaven, the Ocean Star,
guide of the wanderer, here below.
Thrown on life's surge, we claim thy care,
save us from peril and from woe …

The room fills up with the scent of lilac,
some of the boys are already wearing sandals.
Maybe it's just that the school year is almost over,
that the evenings are longer, that
the sun is out after months of cold and rain,
but it feels like the air itself is changed.

Carey sings out with the best of us,
his deep voice holding everything together,
his eyes closed, his shoulders dropped.
It won't last, I know that, we all know that,
but for just a moment, and I don't know why,
I'm willing to give him the benefit of the doubt.

Day of Misrule

The classroom floors are made from blocks of wood,
all locked together in a pattern.
This is called parquet, Carey told us that
and I looked it up. On the last day before
we break up, we polish the floors.
Organised chaos, the red-headed Brother says.

Brother Nolan, I found out his name,
talking to one of the other teachers, both of them laughing.
Next day we find out what it means. Bring in
an old pair of socks tomorrow, Carey says.
We know from the lore what this means,
we're looking forward to it.

First we pile the desks out into the corridor,
banging and shouting, screeching the metal legs
on the terrazzo. Then he picks out a handful of boys
and with cloths and tins of dark polish
we cover the floor with a sticky wax.
Out to the yard then for an hour, the joy of play

while others are still locked in their classrooms,
waiting their turn. Now comes the best bit:
we fit the socks over our shoes and then
we go skating all over the floor, over and back,
bumping and shoving, laughing our heads off
as we bring up a fine, hard, glossy shine.

Then we carry the desks back, careful now,
not wanting to make scratches, proud of our work.
We tiptoe in and settle, unusually quiet,

the windows wide open to let the smell out.
I like the smell of polish, I love it at home
when Mam polishes the hall with Cardinal Red.

Carey is rocking backwards and forwards
at the top of the room, his arms folded,
looking over the top of his glasses.
For a long time he says nothing and we wonder
what's up. He's making us uneasy, he knows this,
I can tell from the upturned corners of his mouth.

What should we do now, lads, he asks.
We're not that stupid, nobody answers him. Silence.
I suppose, he says, I suppose that's it for the year,
what do you think? A different silence now
as we try to work out what's coming. There's a funny look
on his face when he waves his arms at us suddenly

and says: go on then, what's keeping ye?
Go home, away out with ye, enjoy the summer. Go on!
Nobody moves, we all just look at him, shocked,
then Murray stands up, looks Casey in the eye and says:
about time, too. Get out, says Carey, laughing,
get out of my sight. And out we all rush.

A Surprise

New class, new teacher, change in point of view.
This one, I note, is interested, asks real questions
and listens to answers. What does your father do?
Lorry driver, docker, unemployed. Factory worker.
Come Friday the collection stays in the box.
I have a new word to ponder, torpor.
Rain in the afternoon, room overheated, we drone
a verse in bored, lifeless chorus then, suddenly:
you, Sprague, what do you want to be when you leave here?
I don't hear the answers as he reels in the others,
realise with a soft shock what mine will be.
So, when he asks, I hold his look and say 'A writer, Sir.'
Trailing home I will wonder, which of us was the more surprised?

Fire Down Town

Fire down in the flat part of the city, ball of smoke
against grey sky, flame fitful at the heart.
Halfway through the afternoon class. He catches me
staring hungrily out the window; my hand flexes,
I half-rise from the desk but he says,
'Right then, off you go. Read it out to us on Monday.'
I suspect a trap, hesitate, then realise he means it.

Suttons, the coal merchants, big block of offices
at the end of the South Mall. Traffic is in a mess,
the fire engines every which way in the road.
Tall helmets over the heads of the murmuring crowd.

Adept from the Sunday matches, I wriggle through
shouldering men. The smell is of burning paper,
blistering wood. Few flames, a crown of smoke
and steam from the ranked windows. A disappointment
in its way. Already they are rolling away some hoses.
From a match report, remembered, I pluck 'thwarted'.
And then I think, well, I can always make stuff up.

Scholarship Class

Scholarship class, we come back after school,
the room, the corridors, bright-lit against night outside.
Not all of us, I think, looking around me, listing the ones
Who've decided they've had enough, they won't go on.

The night calms us, we're steady and quiet for the most part,
first intimations that this is not forever, that life goes on after.
The *Schol* is the gate to Secondary, to good jobs, the Civil Service,
    teaching …
The lights are hard and sharp against the black dark outside.

Always there is a slight crackle in the air, a flicking nerve,
something like what you feel when you're robbing orchards,
and then one night, running home, it hits me:
those absent boys, maybe it isn't their choice,
maybe they're leaving early because they have to.
Not all of us are equally poor.

That Look

We hate them on principle, the teachers; we know they don't like us,
they suffer us as a penance, some of them actively despise us.
You don't have to be a genius to work this out, we agree among
    ourselves.
We have them all figured out: *Fuckface. Born Drunk. Madman.*
Pocket the Box. Gorgeous George. Names handed on with fearful relish.
Our lurid fantasies of revenge, whisper-shared in the yard at break.
Hurley's all right, Dan Sprague says, he's decent. We agree an exception.

This one we haven't a nickname for, the red-headed Brother who'll
    see us out.
Nolan, known only as that. He's working his way down the row,
asking what Confirmation names we mean to take. 'Joseph, Brother.'
An eyebrow lifts, 'Why Joseph'? Sudden attentive stillness.
'Because, Brother, Saint Joseph is the patron saint of workers.'
He turns away sharply, not quite quick enough to resume the mask.
Afterwards I will wonder, did he mean me to catch that look?

A Great Silence in the City

The ramp, the tunnel, smell of concrete heating slowly under the sun.
The gates are shut but I long ago learned to slide under — if the
    head fits
the rest will follow. I drag my bag after me, books no longer needed,
a weight to be passed on when I get home. Over my shoulder,
blocking the sun, the high bulk of the Secondary, deep shadowed
    windows,
pillared doorways into who knows what. I shrug it off, the shadow
    and fret —
there will be time for that. A great silence in the city, no thud of
    football,
no drone of traffic, no voice calling high and wide between
    sandstone walls.
Someone comes out of the Laundry by the side door, carrying a
    brown paper parcel,
scuttles away. Now there's a word I like, the move in the very
    sound of it.

Pandemonium earlier, boys exploding in all directions, roaring
    and shouting
and elbowing each other to be out the door and gone, as if none
    of this
had ever happened, door of the past brutally closed. Pandemonium,
demons everywhere — once when a referee had given a free in the
    wrong
direction, describing it all to a neighbour, my father said it:
    'pandemonium
everywhere, skin and hair flying' — and I'd gone to explain what
    it meant, say
that I'd looked it up, but a sudden reluctance came over me, and I
    shut my mouth.

All this in my head when the sun paints holiday on the gable of
    Cahill's shop
and the voice inside says easy now, easy. You will remember this.

I pack it all carefully away: that's that, it's done. That will do for now.

CODA

In the small closed yard …

In the small closed yard boys ricochet
off the walls and bounce off each other,
animal spirits all.

Here the dark women patrol,
each one a gliding mystery.
Some kind, some cruel, all veiled.

Mrs. Ryan is dust, that room is dust
and rubble, under a road somewhere
or in a landfill. The rocking horse,

bright-lit as by lightning in a storm
fades into black. Some of those boys
are already gone, spun into the wind,

over the city they never left.
They fall like snow, like ash, soft
through the rippling music of the bells,

on Shandon Street, St. Mary's Road, Fair Hill,
on Churchfield and Gurranebraher,
on Spangle Hill that became Farranree,

down over the valley of sweet Blackpool.
And I am still walking up Redemption Road,
my hand warm in her warm hand,

thumb under the strap of the schoolbag
snug on my back, a clutch of drawings
to be smoothed out on the kitchen table.

Everyone will say they are very good —
then they'll forget about them, I'll run outside
and everything will go on forever.